THE SOM

France 1916

Chris McNab

Fought astride the River Somme in Picardy, France, in July–November 1916, the Battle of the Somme has a unique place in British military history. By the end of the first day of combat on 1 July, 57,470 British soldiers were dead, wounded or missing. Never before or since has the British Army sustained such losses in a 24-hour period. The French armies fighting on the campaign's right flank also lost 7,000 men. The fact that the shocking toll in human life brought advances measured, in many places, only in yards rather than miles, if any distance at all, compounded the tragedy.

Yet as this book explores, the opening day of the Somme was just the beginning of a campaign that lasted for more than four months, and was as tragic for the Germans as it was for the British and the French. It was a battle aimed at bleeding the enemy white through a strategy of attrition, and at breaking the deadlock on the Western Front. Whether it achieved these goals in any significant measure has been a matter of argument for historians ever since the guns fell silent on the Western Front in 1918. Over the years, the campaign has also gathered its fair share of popular myths and over-simplifications, many of which we will tackle here. Looking from today's perspective, however, the Somme campaign is remembered chiefly as a landmark of suffering in 20th-century history, a caution about the sheer waste of war in an age of industrial firepower. It is a testimony to the nature and ferocity of this battle that it is still remembered so reverently after nearly a century has passed.

BELOW: British troops march up to the front line, waving their helmets at the photographer. The total death toll for British troops in the First World War numbered more than 800,000.

The Outbreak of War

By the time the Battle of the Somme began in July 1916, war had been raging across Europe for nearly two years. The causes of the conflict lay in the complex system of defensive alliances forged between European states during the 19th and early 20th centuries.

By 1914, Europe was essentially divided into two major military and political blocs. On one side was the Triple Alliance, comprising Germany, the Austro-Hungarian Empire and Italy. Politically opposed to this bloc was the Triple Entente of Britain, France and Russia. The two sides were locked in an arms race from the mid 1890s, which combined with territorial disputes, particularly in the Balkans, meant that war remained a constant possibility.

The flashpoint for conflict came on 28 June 1914. The heir to the Austro-Hungarian throne,

Archduke Franz Ferdinand, was killed in Sarajevo by a Serbian nationalist, Gavrilo Princip. Seeing the assassination as a challenge to its imperial influence in the Balkans, Austria-Hungary issued Serbia with a series of intentionally unacceptable demands. When these were not met, Austria-Hungary declared war on Serbia. What happened next was that the complicated European defensive alliances came into play. Armies were mobilized, and this move was soon accompanied by declarations of war. By 4 August 1914, Germany and Austria-Hungary were at war with Britain, France and Russia.

In the West, the Germans launched a sweeping invasion (a modified version of the Schlieffen Plan – see panel), with five armies driving through Luxembourg and Belgium into northern and western France. The aim was to make a

BELOW: The outbreak of war inspired hundreds of thousands of men to join the armed services. Here police officers attempt to control huge queues into a London recruiting office.

RIGHT: Soldiers of the 1st Battalion, Middlesex Regiment, take shelter from German artillery fire on the Signy–Signets road during the Battle of the Marne, 8 September 1914. Several men were injured and nine horses killed by the shellfire.

BELOW: A stained-glass window in the Montparnasse Cemetery, Paris, depicts the French sacrifice at the Battle of the Marne. Six French field armies and one British army brought the German westward advance to a halt in September 1914.

THE SCHLIEFFEN PLAN

The Schlieffen Plan was a German war plan developed by Count Alfred von Schlieffen, German Chief of Staff between 1891 and 1906. Von Schlieffen tried to tackle the problem of what Germany should do if it found itself in a two-front war with France to the west and Russia to the east. His plan was for German forces to invade northern France via Belgium, then encircle Paris and the main French armies. Once a quick victory over France was achieved, then German forces could be redeployed east to fight the Russians. In 1914, a slightly modified version of the plan was put into action, but tougher resistance from Allied forces took all the movement and direction out of the German offensive, and what was meant to be a quick victory bogged down into static warfare.

huge encirclement of French forces, but the offensive did not go to plan. The French and Belgian armies, and the soldiers of the British Expeditionary Force (BEF), resisted vigorously, stopping the Germans short of Paris at the Battle of the Marne in September. Subsequent German attempts to outflank their opponents to the north resulted in the so-called 'race to the sea' (the Channel coast). Yet a series of bloody battles was actually bringing the war of movement to a halt – the Germans ran out of steam, but the Allies did not have the

strength to push them back. From December 1914, each side began to put down defensive positions, giving birth to a relatively fixed front line that stretched from Flanders in the north to Alsace in the south. It was the need to break this deadlock that would lead directly to the Battle of the Somme.

RIGHT: German troops advance in November 1914. Pre-war German battle plans were based on an infantry advance of about 20 miles (32km) a day, an impossible rate to sustain for long.

Trench Warfare, 1915–16

By the end of 1914, Germany was in possession of most of Belgium and large parts of northern France. Yet there the war in the West seemed to stop. Each side dug elaborate and extensive defensive trench systems, hewn into the soil, mud and rock of the battlefield. The opposing trenches were separated by a short strip of 'no man's land' – typically between 100 and 400 yards (90–365m) wide – and protected by barbed-wire defences, trench mortars, artillery batteries, machine-guns and the rifles of the infantry. Conditions for those living in and fighting from the trenches gradually went from rough to horrendous. Sanitation and food were poor, disease and violent death commonplace and illnesses rife. Yet the trenches undeniably provided protection – most of the war's major battlefield death tolls occurred when troops left the safety of their trench lines to attack across open ground.

The static nature of the Western Front remained essentially unbroken for three years.

Yet both sides invested much effort trying to break the deadlock. The French and the British launched major offensives in the first half of 1915, but the gains were either minimal or temporary. Further Allied and German onslaughts the following September did not change the situation.

Despite the blood being spilt on the battlefield (more than 144,000 British and French casualties in the autumn campaigns alone), by the end of the year the Allies in particular were feeling bullish about the prospects for victory in 1916. The armies of Britain and France were growing to epic proportions. By the end of 1915, France's programme of conscription had brought

ABOVE: German snipers take shots at French infantry during the Battle of Verdun. Casualties from snipers were minimal compared to those from artillery and machine-guns, but the fear of snipers severely restricted movement around the battlefield.

LEFT: A view along a typical British trench on the Western Front. British trenches were usually created in sections called 'firebays', separated by angular 'traverses' designed to protect the occupants of one firebay from shell hits against adjacent firebays.

RECRUITING THE BRITISH ARMY

When Britain went to war in 1914, it did so with a small regular army of just 250,000 men, which soon proved totally insufficient for the scale of the fighting. (Only 150,000 of these men were at first deployed as the BEF.) The Secretary of State for War, Field Marshal Lord Kitchener, implemented a nationwide call for volunteers. Fuelled by patriotism and propaganda, and much social pressure, British men flocked to volunteer for military service in 'Kitchener's New Army'. One million men had enlisted by January 1915;

2.5 million by the end of the year. Recruiters were encouraged to form battalions of local men, the belief being that men who knew each other, or who shared a common background, would fight well together. These units became known as 'Pals' battalions. Their danger was that heavy losses amongst a particular battalion would devastate a local community back home. Yet even with the rush of volunteers, the manpower demands of the war were inexhaustible, and conscription was introduced in early 1916.

more than two million men under arms, and Britain's volunteer recruits swelled the British Army to 2.6 million. Britain's Defence of the Realm Act (DORA) of 1914 also ensured that the British economy and industrial strength were directed into fuelling the massive war effort. This effort became politically charged following the so-called 'shell scandal' of 1915. The British Commander-in-Chief, Sir John French, expressed the view that shortfalls in artillery shell production led directly to the failure of the Allied offensive at Neuve Chapelle in March 1915. The subsequent public outcry not only led to the downfall of the Liberal government in Britain (replaced by a coalition government), but also contributed to French being replaced by Sir Douglas Haig, a commander whose name will forever and controversially be associated with the Battle of the Somme.

ABOVE: During the Battle of the Somme, British troops of the Border Regiment show their talent for earth-working in a front line trench at Thiepval Wood.

BELOW: The Western Front, 1915.

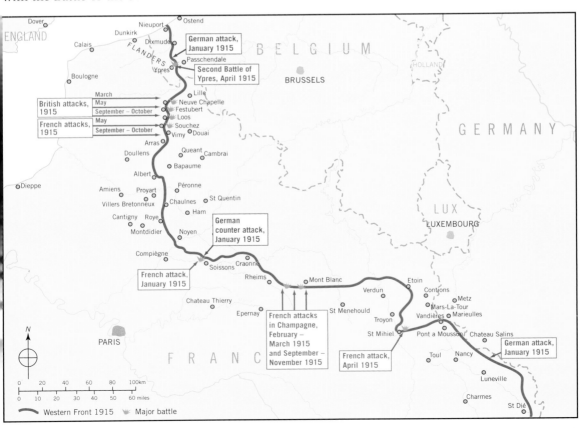

The Commanders

Future generations, rightly or wrongly, would largely lay responsibility for the human cost of the Somme campaign at the feet of its commanders. On the British side, the salient figure was General (later Field Marshal) Sir Douglas Haig. Haig was a model of Victorian certainty and inner steel. He had tremendous confidence in his own judgement – he once remarked that 'I know quite well that I am being used as a tool in the hands of Divine Power.' Haig's leadership, however, has been judged as rather unimaginative. He was at heart a cavalryman, believing in the moral spirit of the charge to break the enemy. His other method, however, was simple attrition – grind down the enemy until he gave way.

Ranked above Haig was the Secretary of State for War, Herbert Kitchener, yet his authority was somewhat bypassed by the appointment in December 1915 of Sir William Robertson as Chief of the General Staff. Robertson was a solid Haig supporter, and they, rather than Kitchener, would be the driving forces behind the Somme strategy and its execution.

On the French side, the Commander-in-Chief of the army was Joseph Joffre. Like Haig, Joffre was a man who led as much by character as by strategic thought. Although he was responsible for the pre-war Plan XVII, a failed and costly attempt to attack Germany and recapture Alsace-Lorraine in August 1914, he restored his reputation by stopping the German advance at the first Battle of the Marne the following September.

RIGHT: Sir Douglas Haig, commander of the British Expeditionary Force from December 1915. Haig could be suspicious of the value of modern weaponry, even once stating that he found the machine-gun a 'much overrated weapon'.

BELOW: A French observation balloon during the Battle of the Marne, 1914. The crew of the balloon typically transmitted messages to the ground by semaphore, although occasionally they would use radio.

Another French leader who would be central to the Battle of the Somme was Marshal Ferdinand Foch. A good indicator of Foch's tough mentality is the words he spoke in September 1914, when as commander of the French Ninth Army he fought to contain the German advance: 'Hard pressed on my right. My centre is yielding. Impossible to manoeuvre. Situation excellent. I attack.' In October he was given command of the northern group of French armies, which would take part in the Battle of the Somme. He held this position, with steadily eroded reputation, until the end of 1916.

Looking across no man's land to the Germans, the overarching German commander was the Chief of Staff, General Erich von Falkenhayn. Here was a forceful and war-hungry leader. He had moments of insight and brilliance, and had led Germany to big victories on the Eastern Front against the Russians in 1915. After that, his reputation swung in the balance, dented by the Verdun horror (see page 9) then somewhat restored by campaigns in other theatres. Falkenhayn also predicted an Allied offensive in 1916, although at Arras, not on the Somme. More locally, the key German commanders around the Somme were General Max von Gallwitz and General Fritz von Below, who between them commanded the main armies that would face the Allied onslaught in July 1916.

LEFT: General Ferdinand Foch had been in French Army service for more than 40 years by the time the First World War broke out in 1914. By the end of the war he had risen to the position of Chief of the General Staff.

COMMAND AND CONTROL

One of the great problems of First World War commanders was how to control their formations in real time. Commanders generally occupied command posts well behind the lines, and therefore struggled to obtain timely information about battlefield events. The most high-speed system was the field telephone, but shellfire frequently cut the lines. Messenger dogs and pigeons provided alternative, much slower, communications, but the former were often killed by shells and snipers and the latter were very weather sensitive. Finally, and most common, were human runners, both slow and vulnerable. Little wonder, therefore, that commanders often took decisions based on out-of-date information, and issued commands that, in some instances, didn't reach the front line for 24 hours.

German infantry transport carrier pigeons in specially designed crates along the battlefront in 1915. Pigeons could only be trained to fly to a fixed and known point, such as a headquarters post.

Planning the Offensive

The seeds of the Battle of the Somme were sown in December 1915. Frustrated by the deadlock into which the Western Front had descended, the Allies gathered together in conference on 6 December at Chantilly, a pretty town north of Paris, to discuss their offensive options for 1916. Rather than launch their own individual campaigns, the Allies agreed to commit to simultaneous offensives on multiple fronts – the Western Front, Eastern Front and Italian Front. The aim was to overwhelm Germany's capacity to respond to attacks from so many different directions.

On the the Western Front, the British and French armies would launch a massive combined assault around the River Somme. The location, in Picardy, was something of a compromise – Haig wanted to launch an attack further to the north in Flanders (the Ypres salient), but the Somme was eventually chosen as it was simply

the junction between the French and British armies. The offensive would be led by the French, who planned to commit 39 divisions compared to Britain's 25 divisions, and was scheduled for mid August 1916.

On 21 February 1916, however, everything changed. The Germans launched a huge offensive further south against Verdun, drawing

ABOVE: A German flamethrower, captured during the Somme campaign. In total, the Germans conducted more than 650 major flamethrower attacks during the war.

BELOW: German soldiers man a trench gun on the Somme. In addition to artillery, the Germans on the Somme front had emplaced more than 1,000 machine-guns by the time the offensive began on 1 July 1916.

LEFT: German dugouts were masterpieces of engineering. Seen here are the steps leading down to the German underground shelter at Bernafay Wood, near Montauban.

BELOW: A French soldier prepares to throw a hand grenade from a trench during the Battle of Verdun. He holds a small shield in his left hand, to protect himself from snipers.

away prodigious volumes of French manpower to fuel the battle (see panel). The fighting at Verdun ran from February to December, and radically changed the priorities of the Somme offensive. From being in a supporting role, the British would now have to take the lead, although French forces would still be heavily involved. Verdun also caused the British to be ready to attack six weeks earlier than had been originally planned.

In essence, the plan involved a massive preparatory artillery bombardment of the German lines, followed by attacks from the British Fourth Army and the French Sixth Army across a broad front. The British Third Army would contribute a limited diversionary attack at the northern end of the main attack front. (Later in the actual campaign, in September, the French Tenth Army would also join the battle.) The major objective for the British was the town of Bapaume, while the French aimed for the town of Péronne. If a breakthrough could be achieved, the Allied forces could then attack north into the German flank, and cavalry could surge through to exploit the gap. As with all plans made in war, the reality of actual battle would be very different.

THE BATTLE OF VERDUN

The Battle of Verdun was one of the greatest, and most destructive, battles of the First World War. Von Falkenhayn launched his attack on Verdun on 21 February 1916, the main German objective being little more than an epic struggle of attrition that would cause the French Army, in von Falkenhayn's words, to 'bleed to death'. The battle was one of almost unparalleled violence – even today the landscape remains heavily modified by the devastating artillery bombardments. Although the Germans drove back the French front line several miles between February and July, the French Army prevented the fall of Verdun itself, and retook some of the lost ground in the autumn. The battle dragged on until December 1916. When it finally ceased, the fighting had bled the German Army as much as the French, and cost 300,000 lives on each side.

Preparing the Way

Artillery was to pave the way for the Somme offensive. On 24 June 1916, a thunderous artillery barrage opened up from the British and French lines, and kept going until 1 July. During the week-long bombardment, more than 1,500 guns pumped 1.7 million shells into the German front lines.

The German soldiers enduring such a bombardment faced the ultimate trauma. A German medical officer wrote: 'Day and night, the shells came upon us. Our dugouts crumbled. They would fall on top of us and we'd have to dig ourselves and our comrades out. Sometimes we'd find them suffocated or smashed to pulp ... Even the rats became hysterical and came into our flimsy shelters to seek refuge from this terrific artillery fire.'

Yet while undeniably dramatic, the artillery fire did not have the intended results of clearing away the German barbed-wire and crushing the fighting power of the defenders. There were several reasons for this. First, the explosions often had the effect of simply redistributing the barbed-wire, rather than destroying it. Second, the effect of the fire was limited by the high number of shells that didn't explode. This situation was a particular issue for the British because of the delay in gearing civilian industries to military production, and problems in obtaining high-quality raw materials. A full 30 per cent of the shells fired during the British Somme barrage didn't explode. Even worse, 25 per cent of the guns malfunctioned owing to poor design or deficient construction standards.

A third major reason for the limited effects of the bombardment was the sheer size of the battlefront.

FIRST WORLD WAR ARTILLERY

The First World War was an artillery war. At the beginning of the conflict, the principal artillery pieces were field artillery guns, typically of around a 3-inch (75-mm) calibre. Designed to be towed into action by horses, and used at relatively close ranges and flat trajectories, they were soon found to have limited effect against trench works. Deep trenches could only be penetrated by shells falling at steeper angles, and consequently trench mortars and medium and heavy howitzers became more central to artillery barrages. By autumn 1915, artillery bombardment plans consisted of concentrating as many artillery pieces as possible against enemy lines, with gun ranges running from about 2 miles (3km) for light guns up to around 7 miles (11km) for heavy artillery. There were typically four types of artillery shell – shrapnel, high-explosive, gas and smoke.

BELOW: Canadian troops on the Somme fit bayonets to their Short Magazine Lee-Enfield (SMLE) rifles before going 'over the top'. The bayonet had more value for morale than in combat, but it was also a handy utility tool.

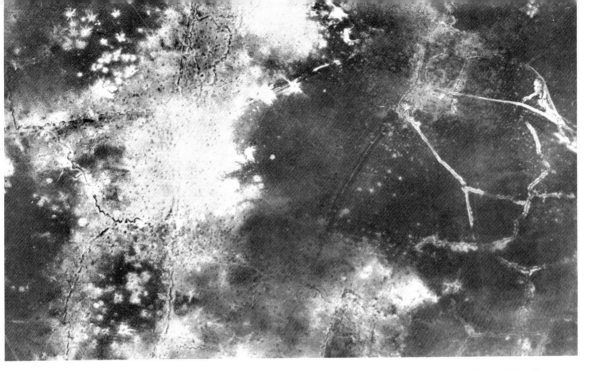

ABOVE: An aerial photograph shows British artillery impact craters and explosions clustered around a German forward trench position on the Somme, just before the British offensive began.

The attack frontage was more than 20 miles (32km) long, and the German defences were several lines deep. Furthermore, the Germans had built numerous protective dugouts, some 30–40 feet (9–12m) deep in the chalky ground, and most withstood the hurricane of fire.

Indications that things weren't going quite to plan came around 28 June. Patrols sent out at night to examine the German defences found that the results of the bombardment weren't as effective as expected. Because of this, and because of recent heavy rain, the barrage was extended for another couple of days, pushing back the attack date to 1 July. When that day came, the British soldiers would find out the true strength of the German defences.

ABOVE: Poor ammunition and deficient manufacturing standards could make some artillery pieces more dangerous to their crews than the enemy. Here a German howitzer has been destroyed by a barrel burst.

RIGHT: A British gun crew man and fire a 6-inch (15.2-cm) howitzer. The men on the left are unpacking the shells and setting the fuses in the nosecaps, making the shells into live munitions ready for firing.

The First Day, 1 July 1916

D awn broke over the Somme on 1 July 1916 with a final intensification of the week-old Allied artillery bombardment, the British guns firing for an hour at a combined rate of 3,500 rounds per minute. In addition, between 0720 and 0730 hours, ten explosive-filled mine works, dug beneath the German trenches, were detonated. The largest of the mines contained more than 60,000lbs (27,270kg) of ammonal explosive, and they literally lifted large sections of German trenches into the air. Two minutes after the last mine detonated, the whistles blew and thousands of British and French infantry surged from their trenches into the attack.

The Somme attack plan broke down as follows. General Edmund Allenby's Third Army was to make a diversionary attack in the far north of the battlefield around Gommecourt. Its purpose was to draw away fire from the main attack further south, made by General Sir Henry Rawlinson's Fourth Army from just east of Serre to Maricourt. Waiting to exploit any British breakthrough was Lieutenant-General Sir Hubert Gough's Reserve Army. The French Sixth and Tenth Armies, meanwhile, were to attack in the south below Maricourt.

Tens of thousands of Allied soldiers now stepped out of their trenches into no man's land, in good visibility with no element of surprise –

ABOVE: A German MG08 machine-gun crew. The soldier at the front grips the water container that fed cooling water into the barrel jacket via the visible hose; the water prevented the barrel from overheating during heavy fire.

BELOW: A powerful image of British soldiers going 'over the top'. On the Somme, many troops died the instant they left the safety of their trenches.

ABOVE: German soldiers lie dead on the Somme battlefield. It is likely that all these men were killed by a single shell-strike or rapid barrage of shells.

WALKING TACTICS

In terms of tactics, it is often noted by historians how the British soldiers at the Somme were given prior instructions to cross no man's land at a walking pace. Such were indeed Rawlinson's instructions, but he had his reasons. First, it was expected that all German resistance would have been crushed by the artillery bombardment – fast manoeuvre was not required. Second, many soldiers were carrying around 66lbs (30kg) of kit, so anything more than walking pace was scarcely possible. Finally, a high percentage of troops had limited training in the tactics of fire and manoeuvre, so keeping them together at walking pace seemed the best way of achieving unified movement across the battlefield. However, many individual units ignored the stipulations and moved at a more sensible faster pace to cross no man's land.

the blowing of the mines and the cessation of the bombardment told the Germans they were coming. German machine-gunners, who had emerged from their dugouts and quickly set up their weapons, and largely untouched German artillery now delivered slaughter on an industrial scale. Entire battalions were almost wiped out in minutes (32 battalions lost more than 500 men each on 1 July). Those who managed to cross no man's land often found themselves stuck against uncut barbed wire, where they were picked off by accurate rifle fire.

In a devastating day of killing, the British sustained 57,470 casualties, of which 19,240 were fatalities. Nor was the loss for any great gain. British attacks in the north made no progress at all, while the furthest British penetrations made by Fourth Army were about a mile (1.6km) in depth at their greatest extent further south, taking the villages of Montauban and Mametz. In the far south, by contrast, the French armies actually exceeded most of their Day One objectives, being better supported by artillery and their infantry using more sensible and effective tactics of surprise and manoeuvre.

By the time night fell on 1 July 1916, the Somme battlefield was choked with British dead and wounded, the worst one-day loss in British history. And yet, this was just the beginning – fighting would continue for most of the year.

RIGHT: About 40,000 British soldiers were injured on the first day of the Battle of the Somme. Here we see a typical British aid station, the wounded laid out on the ground while they wait for triage or treatment.

Pushing On, 2–22 July

The terrible first-day casualties of the Battle of the Somme had by no means discouraged Haig or Rawlinson from pushing on. But the German Second Army was also hurting. Its own losses had been severe, and it had been forced to make a substantial withdrawal in the south of the line, as the French maintained a good advance along the Bray–Péronne road. The British also fought off German counter-attacks at Montauban on 2 July, the same day on which they captured Fricourt. Sensing danger, the German high command drew away troops from Verdun to reinforce the Somme sector.

Various points along the front line became pockets of constant fighting. For example, although the British had taken the village of Mametz, there was a large area of woodland to the north-east that remained in German hands. On 7 July, the 38th (Welsh) Division began an assault to clear Mametz Wood, supported by French gas artillery attacks. When the British finally secured the area, on 12 July, the 38th Division had lost 190 officers and 3,803 other ranks dead or wounded.

A second major 'Big Push' took place on 14 July, reaching High Wood and Delville Wood, but then the battle stagnated and this successful day was followed by two months of only slow and costly progress on the British attack front. It was during this period that the 9th (Scottish) Division took Longueval, on 14 July. The South African Brigade, which was attached to the division, then began a terrible struggle to clear the tree-splintered wasteland that was now Delville Wood, a process that was not fully completed until near the end of August and cost the brigade 2,300 men.

ABOVE: The Welsh Dragon Monument at Mametz Wood remembers the sacrifice of the 38th (Welsh) Division in the area in July 1916. The dragon is shown tearing at barbed wire.

BELOW: A British gun crew prepare to load and fire a 12-inch (30.5-cm) howitzer during the battle for Thiepval. The shell bears the graffiti 'For Fritz', a negative reference to the Germans.

LEFT: A dramatic artwork, taken from the French magazine *L'Illustration* in 1918, shows a French raiding party working its way through the knee-deep mud of the Somme battlefield.

The British were moving forward during this period, but the gains were often measured in yards and the casualties were horrendous. Other objectives remained out of reach, however. Four British attacks towards the village of Pozières in mid July all ran aground, and the fortified village of Thiepval – less than a mile (1.6km) from the 1 July start line – remained in German hands by dogged resistance.

LEFT: Siegfried Sassoon, one of the greatest of the First World War poets, was involved in the fighting at Mametz Wood in July 1916.

A LETTER OF CONDOLENCE

The following excerpts are from a letter written to the father of Second Lieutenant Kenneth Macardle, 17th Battalion, the Manchester Regiment, who was killed on 8–9 July during the Somme offensive. His body was never found.

```
                            In The Field
                               14-7-16
Dear Mr Macardle
I regret very much to have to inform you
that your son has been missing since
the recent fighting in Trones Wood. The
wood changed hands several times, and
it is possible that he was captured when
our regiment was compelled to evacuate
the wood. If this is the case, you will
doubtless hear from him soon .... The
wood was shelled so heavily by both
sides that it was almost impossible
for anyone to live in it, and I have
very grave anxiety concerning the fate
of your son .... I hope sincerely that
he is still alive, but I am afraid the
chances are slight. Whether alive or
killed in action, I shall always be glad
I have know him, and I assure you you
may be very proud to have so gallant a
son.
        Yours sincerely
        C L Macdonald, Major
          17th. Manch. Regt.
```

Attrition, 22 July–14 September

As the Somme campaign moved into late July, many of the objectives staked out for the first days of the offensive remained stubbornly elusive. One of those objectives was the Pozières Ridge. It was essential that the Allies take this high ground if they were to continue the advance further up the Albert–Bapaume road. The village itself was also a fortified outpost in front of the German second-line trenches: take Pozières, and these trenches could be threatened. Thousands of casualties had already been sustained in the push on Pozières, but between 16 and 21 July the Allies gathered their strength for another attempt.

This attack began on 22 July, and the Australian troops of Gough's Reserve Army bore much of the brunt of the fighting, as well as the British 48th (South Midland) Division. The combat was brutal and chaotic against well-entrenched defensive positions – the Germans had used the lull since the last attack to emplace their machine-guns in shell holes. Pozières was mostly taken by the end of 23 July. Yet frenzied German counter-attacks and determined resistance from their second-line trenches meant that by the time the battle was won by the Allies on 7 August, the Australians alone had suffered 23,000 casualties.

Such difficult gains were repeated along the whole front. Delville Wood was finally cleared on 27 August. At High Wood near Flers, the wearing process of attack and counter-attack went on until the Allies took the area on 15 September (see pages 18–19); the objectives of Ginchy and Guillemont were also secured

ABOVE: At the battle for Pozières Ridge, Australian troops load a 9.45-in (24-cm) trench mortar, a weapon known affectionately as the 'flying pig'.

BELOW: Autumnal rains turned the Somme battlefield into a sea of mud. Horses suffered as much as men, and often died from lack of suitable fodder in the appalling conditions.

ABOVE: Following the battle of Guillemont, personnel from the Royal Army Medical Corps search the clothing and packs of the dead for identification and personal effects, the latter to be sent home to relatives.

AN INFANTRYMAN'S WAR DIARY

The following extract is from the war diary of Australian infantryman Oswald Blows, dated 29 July 1916. Here Blows describes his part of the front line around Pozières:

```
Our firing line - a captured battered
trench, was about 400 yds from the Hun,
& our hopping-off trench, in front in
no man's land. The Hun's trenches were
on the ridge almost, of a gently rising
slope. We were at this time between the
wholly ruined Pozières village, & the
Ridge, our sector taking the road from
Albert for Baupaume. The stench was
bad from the dead; we'd passed many on
our way. We were to make our H.Q. in a
shell-hole - 100 yds in rear of [where]
our men were to attack, & close to some
ruined houses - probably a street once.
We fixed up wires to every company, but
they were never used. Arrangements were
for our Artillery to open up at mid-
night, & bombard until 12.16, then our
Infantry to rush the first trench, while
barrage lifted & bombarded the 2nd line
for 6 minutes, then barrage to lengthen,
& us to take second trench, & push as
far as possible - to make an outpost at
least of the ruins of an old windmill
near the road.
```

by this date. The French, meanwhile, pushed their front further forward, particularly at the junction between the French Sixth Army and the British Fourth Army. By 15 September, the French had moved past Maurepas, and were also supporting the British drive eastward. In fact, the French advance had become limited by the British struggles to the north – they could not push too far forward beyond the British without creating an exposed flank.

By now Haig was under pressure. The British government was beginning to question why advances of a few miles at best had cost tens of thousands of lives. They also wanted to know if an end was in sight. Haig assured them that the enemy was buckling, and a further concerted effort would break their will.

BELOW: Soldiers of the 1st Australian Division pose after their hard-fought victory at Pozières. Some are wearing captured German helmets, and a Lewis light machine-gun is displayed in the bottom left of the picture.

Tanks and Trenches, 15 September–1 October

The French in particular were, by mid September 1916, acutely aware of the fact that the Somme was becoming another grinding mill for its manpower. Marie Émile Fayolle, the commander of the French Sixth Army, had remarked that 'This battle has ... always been a battle without an objective. There is no possibility of breaking through. And if a battle is not for breaking through, what is its purpose?' Haig was coming under increasing criticism for the campaign's slow progress, but insisted that the Allies had to maintain pressure to see the desired results.

There were admittedly some technological advances brought to the battle from mid September onwards. In artillery, for example, the Allies had by now achieved a greater mastery of the 'creeping barrage', delivering a walking wall of artillery fire behind which the infantry advanced. The advantage of the creeping barrage was that it gave the enemy less time to prepare their defence once the barrage had passed. The other great innovation was the tank. Crude, boxy, unreliable and poorly armoured the Mk I tank (see panel) was nevertheless thrown into action in mid September, and with decent psychological if not practical effect.

Major objectives for the Fourth Army's 15 September offensive included Flers, Gueudecourt, Lesboeufs and Morval.

ABOVE: A Mk I tank. The two wheels at the rear acted as a 'steering tail', although these were actually one of four ways in which the driver could steer the tank.

BELOW: A dramatic image from the battle of Flers–Courcelette in mid September 1916 shows the early-morning sky slashed by artillery fire in preparation for an attack on Thiepval.

Using 36 tanks (13 others had broken down before the battle began), the Allies took the first two of these objectives on 15 September (the troubled High Wood was also taken), advancing the line between Flers and Courcelette by about 2,000 yards (1,800m). Not until the end of the month, however, would Lesboeufs and Morval be captured.

Most of the advances were in the central part of the line, but towards the end of September the focus shifted to the left flank. It focused

WORDS FROM THE BATTLEFRONT

These extracts are from the war diary of Second Lieutenant Harold Cope, written during his time fighting in and around Delville Wood. As his diary indicates, Cope was seriously injured on 7 August:

AUGUST 5 1916 ————————
Day-break. Cpt. Rchdsn. & Mahoney came along. Got men clearing trench for a while, then they rested. I got bit of sleep. Quiet day. Along to other officers, Roy, Matthews, Hamilton & Cptns. Something to eat. In evng. moved 16 platoon along to form strong pt. Heavy shelling near. Took M.G. down. At last. 12 a.m.–1 a.m. 1 shell caught the men. Morris killed, L/Cpl. Thorne, Lawson, Pounder wounded. G. bandaged, latter explored trench, got stretchers & guide.

AUGUST 7 1916 ————————
Signallers & Bombers about. Heavy shelling all morn. Lay in dug-out cov. with shield. Hot. Over top 4.51 wounded Fainted. Drssd To Fld Drsg St HQ. then Field Amb & on Car by & to Dernancourt Bad nt.

ABOVE: An exhausted British soldier sleeps in a trench at Thiepval. His rifle is the 0.303-inch (7.7-mm) SMLE, which in capable hands could deliver 15 shots per minute.

ABOVE: Piles of German stick grenades, helmets and other equipment were left behind after St Pierre-Divion was captured by the British 39th Division on 13 November 1916.

killing was carried out primarily with bolt-action rifles, such as the German 7.92mm Mauser Gewehr 98, the British 0.303-inch Short Magazine Lee-Enfield (SMLE) and the French 8mm Lebel, all capable of taking vicious bayonets (the standard British bayonet had a 17-inch/43-cm blade). The rifles were reliable and accurate, and, with telescopic sights, excellent sniping weapons. They could, however, be unwieldy in the confines of trench combat, when infantry often resorted to pistols, but also the medieval brutality of crudely spiked clubs, sharpened spades and other hand-held weapons. The most influential infantry weapon was the machine-gun, such as the German MG08, the British Vickers and Lewis guns, and the French Hotchkiss. The German MG08, for example, could engage targets at 2,000 yards (2,000m) at a rate of 400 rounds per minute. A British

soldier, Lance Corporal H. Bury, who fought on 1 July, remembered that 'We were able to see our comrades move forward in an attempt to cross no man's land, only to be mown down like meadow grass.' Such sights would burn themselves into the memories of the survivors, continuing the trauma of the Somme well after the battle concluded.

Last Gasp, 1 October–18 November

By the autumn and winter of 1916, exhaustion hung like a pall over the Somme battlefield. Haig remained publicly buoyant. The British had made some headway in the September offensives, and in the wider war Romania had changed sides to the Allies in August. Falkenhayn's replacement as Chief of Staff by Paul von Hindenburg suggested a German war leadership in increased disarray. October 1916, therefore, was in Haig's mind an ideal time to intensify the onslaught.

Throughout October and into November the fighting continued along the length of the front. In the far south, the French Sixth Army inched forward its front line south of Péronne, taking Ablaincourt and Fresnes. The biggest British efforts, however, came during the fight for the Transloy Ridges between 1 October and early November, and the climactic struggle for the Ancre Heights from 1 October to 18 November. The battle for Transloy focused on a ridgeline in the Fourth Army sector, where the Germans had constructed new defensive trenches. The British III Corps began its advance on 1 October after a punishing seven-hour bombardment of the German lines. Yet the atrocious weather and tough German defence made advances of mere yards an achievement. Fresh attacks were thrown in on 7, 12, 18 and 23 October and

5 November, but without any substantial returns except for hundreds of dead and wounded.

Fighting for the Ancre Heights in Gough's Reserve Army sector on the left flank of the battlefield was just as much an ordeal, and rumbled on until the very last days of the campaign. The objective was to clear out the remaining German positions and redoubts astride the Ancre River that had been left by the fighting for the Thiepval Ridge. The ground was desperately contested, but by 14 October the Stuff Redoubt and Schwaben Redoubt were finally in Allied hands. Attempts to wrest away the so-called Regina Trench, however, took three weeks of fighting.

On 13 November the last British offensive of the Somme campaign was launched, by the Fifth Army (Gough's now relabelled Reserve Army). The objective was the ground from Beaumont Hamel to Serre. Only the right flank of the attack had any real success, the 51st (Highland) Division capturing Beaumont Hamel on the 13th and the 63rd (Royal Naval) Division capturing Beaucourt in the last major offensive of the Somme battle. But elsewhere the attacks made only minimal gains, in weather that went from bad to atrocious. Serre remained well beyond the British efforts. After some final localized drives, the Battle of the Somme was coming to a close.

LEFT: A desolate view of the Ancre Valley, its trees and landscape blasted by shellfire, and flooded by the winter rains. Bad weather, as much as anything, brought the Somme campaign to a close.

RIGHT: The Somme battlefield, showing stages of advance from 1 July to 15 November 1916.

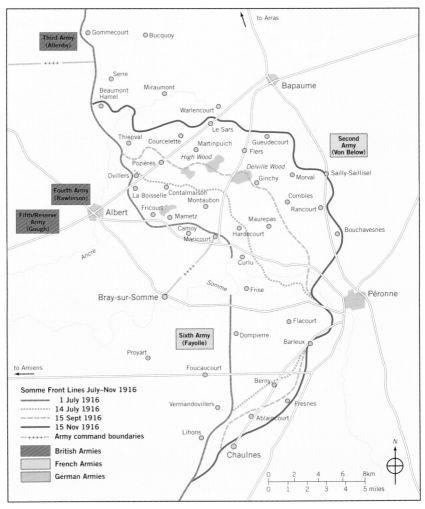

ABOVE: Lieutenant-General Hubert Gough, commander of the Reserve/Fifth Army at the Battle of the Somme, was a traditional British Army cavalry officer and a personal favourite of Douglas Haig.

THE PUBLIC RELATIONS BATTLE

Despite the horror of the Battle of the Somme, public opinion remained largely 'on message' in Britain. While always sombre in tone, many newspaper stories of the fighting could brighten even the most horrible of scenes with a patriotic gloss. For example, an article written by W. Beach Thomas for the *Daily Mirror* (also published in the *Paris Daily Mail*) described dead British soldiers thus: 'Even as he lies on the field he looks more quietly faithful, more simply steadfast than others.' A deeper insight into battlefield conditions came from a silent movie documentary entitled *The Battle of the Somme*. Made by War Office cinematographers Geoffrey Malins and John McDowell, the film depicted scenes such as dead and dying soldiers, and the explosion of some of the mines at the beginning of the offensive. Twenty million viewing tickets were sold, but despite the moving content the public viewed the footage more with reverence than outrage.

A still from Malins and McDowell's documentary *The Battle of the Somme* (1916). The scene shows a man rescuing his comrade, although the wounded man died 30 minutes later.

Success or Failure?

The Battle of the Somme came to an end on 18 November 1916. The onset of winter weather, including the first heavy snows, and simple combat exhaustion made further significant offensive movements impossible. It was time to take stock of what this bloody and prolonged campaign had achieved.

On the face of it, the battle seemed to have brought terrible cost for far too few gains. Total Allied casualties numbered around 660,000, including 200,000 French soldiers. For this cost the maximum advance was around 6 miles (10km), a gain that took more than four months of fighting. At its deepest penetration, the average rate of advance was just 100 yards (91m) per day. To the modern sensibility, such losses for such minor gains seem indefensible. In the second half of the 20th century, many historians labelled Haig and his ilk as virtual monsters, dismissive of the lives of British soldiers and incompetent in command.

The true picture is rather more complicated. The commanders of the First World War were living at a time of fundamental transition in the technology of warfare, with the strength favouring the defence, and they arguably fought the best campaign open to them with the knowledge available. The fact remained that ground had to be crossed to be taken, and that Haig had to maintain offensive pressure to counteract the German squeeze on Verdun. Nor should

THE WIDER WAR

The Battle of the Somme came at a crucial point in the wider war. One of the key reasons why Germany was able to launch its campaign at Verdun in early 1916 was its victories on the Eastern Front against Russia. But Germany was becoming overstretched. Its Austro-Hungarian ally struggled in the Balkans and Eastern Front theatres, and forced Germany to deploy more of its forces there. In June–August 1916, a Russian offensive led by General Aleksei Brusilov produced impressive results in what is today Ukraine, inflicting 1.5 million Austro-Hungarian casualties and obliging the Germans to pull away manpower from Verdun to help stop the tide. In desperate straits, the Germans in February 1917 adopted unrestricted U-boat (submarine) warfare against Allied merchant shipping to Britain. This policy eventually drove the United States to join the Allied cause, a fact that eventually led to Germany's final defeat in 1918.

ABOVE: The German high command. Kaiser Wilhelm II (centre) studies operational plans with Field Marshal Paul von Hindenburg (left) and General Erich Ludendorff. Hindenburg became the German Chief of the General Staff in August 1916.

LEFT: The commune of Roye was devastated by the Somme fighting. Nevertheless, civilian casualties during the Somme offensive remained remarkably low as they had wisely evacuated the battle zones.

RIGHT: German troops on the
Eastern Front in the snow,
wearing white camouflage
uniforms. Roughly 1.5 million
German troops were killed
or wounded fighting Russia
between 1914 and 1917.

we overlook the cost to the Germans, which
was profound. Some 630,000 German soldiers
were casualties, a huge chunk of the available
manpower in 1916.

And yet, returning to the debit side of the
account, the Germans eventually fell back to
the freshly prepared, strong defensive positions
known as the Hindenburg Line, which was
30 miles (48km) shorter than the line they
abandoned, releasing 13 of their divisions from
front line trench holding. The Allies, by contrast,
were left in possession of little more than a
wasteland. Nor did the Germans struggle to man
the new positions, partly through reinvigorated

conscription laws that widened the pool of
available manpower. Nevertheless, many British
commanders and politicians argued that the
very fact that the Germans had been forced to
make a retreat meant that the campaign had
been a success.

Haig certainly never publicly regretted the
Somme campaign. His ideal vision was for a
potentially decisive and massive breakthrough,
and that had evidently failed, whereas Rawlinson
had originally argued for more limited 'bite
and hold' tactics. Whatever the case, the fact
was that an awful lot more war remained to
be fought, and at terrible human cost.

BELOW: The once picturesque Somme/
Picardy region was transformed by war
into a place of total devastation.
It would take decades for the
landscape to recover fully.

Counting the Cost

The cost of the Battle of the Somme was extreme. More than 1.2 million British and Empire (especially Australian, Canadian, New Zealand and South African) and French and German soldiers became casualties over the four and a half months of the campaign. Roughly one third of the casualties were fatalities. The legacy of the deaths and woundings is incalculable, not least amongst the communities back in Britain that had raised local battalions for service.

History has particularly remembered, for example, the 11th (Service) Battalion (Accrington) East Lancashire Regiment, better known as the Accrington Pals. By 24 September 1914, the battalion was 1,100 men strong, half of them recruited purely from Accrington, Lancashire, and the other half from nearby towns. The first major action fought by the battalion was on 1 July 1916, during the attack on Serre. Some 720 Accrington Pals participated in the attack, and witnesses likened their destruction to corn being cut down at harvest time. By the end of the day, 584 of the men were dead, wounded or missing. Back in Britain, the Accrington community was plunged into mourning, as it essentially lost almost an entire generation of its menfolk.

LEFT: Approximately 31,000 German soldiers were taken prisoner during the Somme offensive. Here Germans captured at Beaumont Hamel are kept in a crude barbed wire enclosure.

BELOW: British soldiers remember a dead comrade in a simple battlefield burial. Very few British bodies were repatriated home; most went into mass graves or crude, improvised war cemeteries.

Such terrible losses were repeated time and time again at the Somme. Yet, to put it into perspective, the first-day losses of the campaign were truly unique, the greatest one-day casualty figures in British military history. After that, the casualty tolls averaged several thousand troops per day – still horrifying, but not unusual for a major campaign. Such observations do not, of course, belittle the deaths and wounds of more than a million men.

The wounded, many of whom had limbs amputated, began an uncertain future trying to fit back into the civilian world. In Britain, all ex-service amputees qualified for free artificial limbs, but the sheer numbers of victims meant that demand was generally ahead of supply. In 1915 the opening of the Queen Mary's Hospital, Roehampton (London), which specialized in making and fitting artificial limbs, had helped improve the output, but the Somme stretched the system beyond coping point. The limbless served as a visible reminder to the British public of the profound cost of the war.

Of course, the Battle of the Somme was just one of the many low points of the First World War. In 1917, for example, the Third Battle of Ypres (Passchendaele) between 31 July and 6 November cost about 300,000 Allied and 400,000 German casualties, the Allies paying for each yard of front gained with about 30 lives.

The experience and the associated controversies of this campaign have much in similarity with the Somme. Yet today the Somme name still stands as the ultimate representative of human sacrifice during the First World War.

ABOVE: The length of the Somme battle meant that many bodies killed early in the fighting, but not buried, simply rotted where they fell. Here a German lies where he died outside his shelter at Beaumont Hamel.

BELOW: An official photograph from the Ministry of Information shows two cheerful amputees. The original caption read, rhetorically, 'Are we downhearted?', but thousands of such men faced lifetimes of terrible poverty and social neglect.

BURIAL OF THE DEAD

Death was everywhere during the Somme campaign. Thousands of bodies were left literally where they fell, rotting in the mud, or were buried in crude mass graves. After the campaign, and indeed after the war, special teams of soldiers were tasked with disinterring the now unrecognizable bodies from the earth, and attempting to identify them from personal effects. In most cases, identification proved impossible, and the names of the missing were simply inscribed on the walls of memorials or ossuaries. On the Thiepval Memorial to the Missing, for example, opened in 1932, are the names of 73,335 British and South African soldiers killed on the Somme, but with no known grave. The other Dominion dead have their own memorials. Nearly 60 per cent of the British dead on the Somme from 1916 have no identified grave. Such anonymity is one of the key reasons why Britain today has so many war memorials – with no bodies to bury, families created their own stone and marble centres of grief.

The Battlefield Today

The Somme battlefield today is a place of peace, but also one of emotional pilgrimage for thousands of people interested in this moment in history. Major destinations for visitors are the many war cemeteries and battlefield memorials, such as the German War Cemetery at Fricourt (17,027 burials), the Newfoundland Memorial Park near the village of Beaumont Hamel and numerous sites maintained by the Commonwealth War Graves Commission (CWGC).

Yet there are other legacies to the events of 1916. Thousands of unexploded shells and mines still litter the landscape, many simply lying on the surface of ploughed fields and in woodlands. More than 50 tonnes of such munitions are unearthed every year. They remain a danger, and kill farmers and bomb disposal experts to this day. Alongside the iron legacies, however, are the bodies of long-dead men still being recovered from the soil. In rare cases, their remains are identified after decades of being forgotten, typically from scraps of official papers or even DNA evidence. For example, a body discovered by tourists in 1998, lying by the Lochnagar mine crater, was identified in 2000 as 28-year-old Private George Nugent 22/1306 of the 22nd Battalion of the Tyneside Scottish Northumberland Fusiliers. He was killed within minutes of climbing out of his trench on 1 July 1916. Decades after the war, he was finally buried with full military honours. Such individual acts of remembrance remind us that all of the dead of the Somme once breathed, and hoped that they would reach the end of the day alive.

ABOVE: The Thiepval Memorial to the Missing (background left) was designed by Sir Edwin Lutyens, and was unveiled in August 1932. It attracted some controversy during its construction, many veterans feeling that the money could be put to better use.

BELOW: Poppies bloom in the now-peaceful Somme Valley. The flower was eventually adopted as a symbol of remembrance in Britain and the Commonwealth, inspired by the poppies featured in John McCrae's famous war poem, 'In Flanders Fields'.